Now we
Know about...

SAVING WATER
AND ENERGY

Philip Steele

Crabtree Publishing Company
www.crabtreebooks.com

Published in Canada
Crabtree Publishing
616 Welland Avenue,
St. Catharines, Ontario
L2M 5V6

Published in the United States
Crabtree Publishing
PMB 59051,
350 Fifth Avenue, 59th floor
New York, NY 10118

Editors: Belinda Weber, Lynn Peppas, Reagan Miller
Editorial director: Kathy Middleton
Production coordinator: Kenneth Wright
Prepress technician: Kenneth Wright
Studio manager: Sara Greasley
Designer: Trudi Webb
Production controller: Ed Green
Production manager: Suzy Kelly

Picture credits:
Peter Arnold, Inc/Alamy: p. 23 (top)
iStock: front cover (bottom right), p. 4 (top left and bottom left), 6,
    11 (top), 13 (top), 14, 14–15, 15 (bottom), 17, 20 (top), 20 (bin), 21
Shutterstock: front cover (top right and bottom left), back cover, p. 1,
    4 (center and top right and bottom right), 5, 6–7, 7, 8, 9, 10,
    11 (bottom), 13, 15 (top), 16, 18–19, 20 (girl), 22, 23 (bottom)
Hayley Terry: front cover (top left) and throughout

Every effort has been made to trace copyright holders, and we apologize in advance
for any omissions. We would be pleased to insert the appropriate acknowledgments
in any subsequent edition of this publication.

Library and Archives Canada Cataloguing in Publication

Steele, Philip, 1948-
    Saving water and energy / Philip Steele.

(Now we know about)
Includes index.
ISBN 978-0-7787-4723-9 (bound).--ISBN 978-0-7787-4740-6 (pbk.)

    1. Water conservation--Juvenile literature. 2. Energy
conservation--Juvenile literature. I. Title. II. Series: Now we
know about (St. Catharines, Ont.)

TD388.S74 2009   j333.72   C2009-903608-8

Library of Congress Cataloging-in-Publication Data

Steele, Philip, 1948-
    Saving water and energy / Philip Steele.
        p. cm. -- (Now we know about)
    Includes index.
    ISBN 978-0-7787-4740-6 (pbk. : alk. paper) -- ISBN 978-0-7787-4723-9
(reinforced library binding : alk. paper)
    1. Water conservation--Juvenile literature. 2. Water--Waste--Juvenile
literature. 3. Energy conservation--Juvenile literature. I. Title. II. Series.

TD495.S74 2010
333.72--dc22
                                                    2009023311

Published in 2010 by Crabtree Publishing Company

Printed in Canada/062014/TT20140513

Contents

Save it!

People you live with probably tell you not to waste. If everyone started saving instead of wasting, it could make a big difference to Earth.

Shut the door! You are letting out heat!

Switch off the light!

Do not leave appliances such as the TV on!

Turn off the tap!

What should we be saving?

Water is one thing we should work on saving. We need water to live. We should use less fuel to drive cars and heat our houses. Fuels such as oil, gas, and coal are often used to make electricity. When we use less electricity, we use less of these **resources**.

Trees take many years to grow. When the trees in a forest are cut down, it takes many years for new trees to grow.

Talking Point

Will small changes, such as switching off lights, make a difference?

Yes, small changes do make a difference. If everyone on Earth cared about saving resources, it would help. We need to find ways to protect Earth's resources before they run out.

Why should we worry about waste?

Earth is running out of oil and forests are being **destroyed**. This is because we use three times more energy than we did 100 years ago.

WORD WIZARD!
resources
Natural materials such as water, timber, metals, coal, oil and gas are all resources.

5

Precious Water

People and all living things need water to live. We also use water to wash ourselves. We also clean our clothes, dishes, houses, and cars with water.

What else do we use water for?

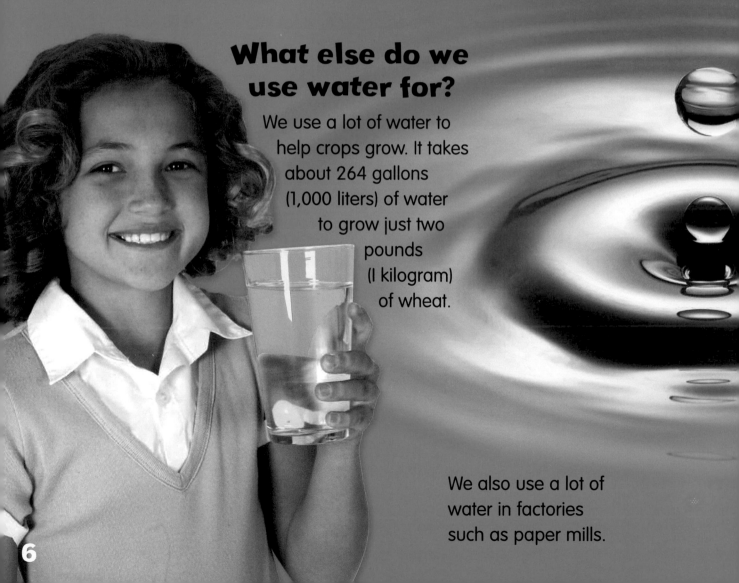

We use a lot of water to help crops grow. It takes about 264 gallons (1,000 liters) of water to grow just two pounds (I kilogram) of wheat.

We also use a lot of water in factories such as paper mills.

6

Where does our water come from?

Earth has a lot of water. Most of it is salt water from oceans, which we cannot drink. A lot of it is ice. Only a small amount of Earth's water can be used by people.

girl carrying water

Do you have tap water?

In many parts of the world people do not have running water in their homes. They have to get water from rivers or wells. In other places, water is saved in **reservoirs**. It is **filtered** and piped into homes.

How can I save water?

Water is easy to save. Turn off taps that drip. Take showers and not baths. If you are waiting for hot water to come from your tap, save the cold water to water your plants.

One in four people on Earth do not have enough clean water.

What is energy?

Energy makes things work or happen. We need energy to start a car or to turn on a computer. We get energy by burning fuels, such as wood, plant materials, or even garbage. We dig up coal, gas, and oil from under the ground.

What happens in a power station?

In many **power stations**, the heat from fuels is used to turn water into steam. This makes **turbines** spin and make electricity.

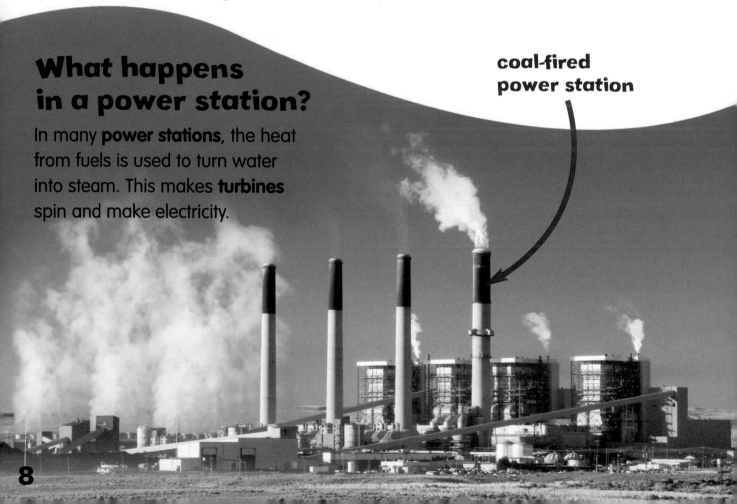

coal-fired power station

We burn wood to make energy with heat. Burning wood creates smoke. Smoke makes pollution.

Do fuels affect Earth?

We use up Earth's resources when we burn fuels. If we use less fuel, we can help save these resources. Some fuels make gases that **pollute** the air. Nuclear fuel makes **radiation** that is dangerous.

Talking Point

How does electricity reach your home from the power station?

Electricity comes into your home through cables and wires. Cables are hung from poles or run underground. Smaller wires in your house carry electricity to your television and other appliances.

WORD WIZARD!
nuclear fuel
Metals such as uranium are changed to make heat

9

From land and water

When we burn wood or coal its energy is used up. Other types of energy can be used again and again. These types of energy are **renewable**. We can use natural heat from deep inside Earth to make electricity in some **power stations**. This is called **geothermal** power.

The center of Earth is boiling hot. It is so hot it can melt rocks. Geothermal power stations turn this heat into electricity.

dam

How can water make power?

The rushing water from rivers or waterfalls can be used to turn turbines. The spinning turbines make electricity. This type of power is called **hydroelectric**.

rushing water

What is wave power?

Waves happen when wind pushes water. Waves are full of energy. Special machines collect this energy and use it to drive turbines.

Wind and Sun

The wind and Sun are natural, renewable energy sources. Both are clean and safe to use.

How can we use wind power?

In the old days windmills did work. They pumped water and ground grain. Today we use them as turbines to make electricity.

Wind turbines are set up over large areas called wind farms. Small wind turbines can make enough electricity for one house.

Wind turbines can work at wind speeds of between 6 and 56 miles per hour (10 and 90 kilometers per hour).

The Sun has given Earth energy for over 4 billion years.

How can we use Sun power?

The heat from the Sun creates solar energy. It can give heat or make electricity in power stations.

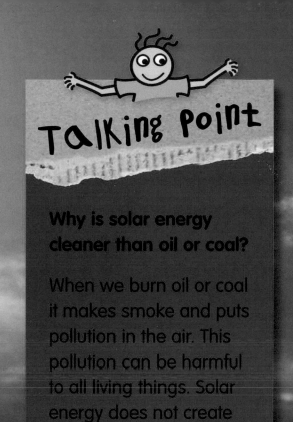

Talking Point

Why is solar energy cleaner than oil or coal?

When we burn oil or coal it makes smoke and puts pollution in the air. This pollution can be harmful to all living things. Solar energy does not create pollution. It is cleaner to use.

What are solar panels?

Special panels can be put on the roofs of buildings. Some panels heat water in the building. Other panels have **cells** that turn sunlight into electricity.

solar panel

Can we save energy at home?

When it is cold, you dress well to keep warm. A layer of clothing holds in your body warmth. This is called insulation. Houses need insulation too. Insulation keeps all the warmth inside the house so it is not wasted.

How can we keep a house warm?

Double, or two, walls keep a house extra warm. Windows with two layers of glass keep the warmth in too. This is called double glazing.

double-glazed window

WORD WIZARD!

insulation
Any material that is used to slow down a change in temperature

An attic often has insulation to stop heat from getting out through the roof.

energy-saving light bulb

Light bulbs such as this have been designed to use less electricity. They last longer, too.

How can we keep our homes cool?

In hot weather a house needs to be cool. Air conditioners use a lot of electricity. Electric fans use less electricity. The best way to keep your home cool is to let air flow through your house. This is called natural **ventilation**.

Talking Point

Does insulation make a difference?

In most houses almost half the heat is lost through the roofs and walls. Good insulation keeps heat from escaping. Less energy is then needed to heat the home. Using less energy saves Earth's resources. It also saves your family money.

15

Indoor savings

Many things we do at home everyday use up a lot of energy. But we can change our ways!

How can you stay cozy in bed?

Even if it is cold, you do not need the heat on overnight. Put an extra blanket on your bed. Insulate yourself!

In the bathroom

Do not leave the tap running when you wash. Use less water in the bath. Shower for a shorter time.

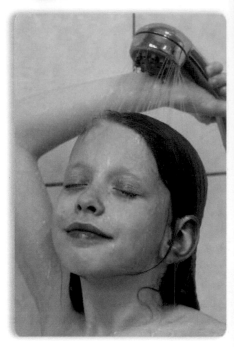

blanket

Washing clothes

Use the economy wash setting on washing machines. Wash small numbers of clothes by hand. Hang your clothes outside to dry. That way you do not need to use the dryer.

Saving electricity

Many homes have a lot of electrical goods, such as radios and computers. Make sure to turn them off when you are not using them. Some electrical outlets can be fitted with timers to cut down on waste.

Turn off the TV!

Talking Point

How can I help save resources?

Think about how you use things around the house. Do not run the tap when you brush your teeth. If you are cold do not turn up the heat. Put on extra clothes, instead.

17

Out and about

Walking or riding your bike to school is great. Our own bodies provide the energy to walk and ride. Other ways of getting about burn up oil or use electricity. This uses up **valuable** resources.

Ride a bike!

Exhaust fumes from cars pollute the air.

How can cars use less fuel?

Some kinds of cars use up a lot of gas. Others use less. Driving at a regular speed can save fuel, too. Sharing car rides with other people uses fewer resources.

Why is it good to use buses and trains?

Public transport burns up fuel, but it carries a lot of people at the same time. If more people use buses or trains, there will be fewer cars on the roads.

Talking Point

How do you spend your free time?

Hobbies are things you like to do in your free time, such as gymnastics, reading, or ballet. You do not need fuel or power to do them. These activities save energy and keep you happy and healthy too.

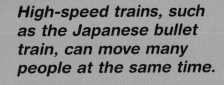

High-speed trains, such as the Japanese bullet train, can move many people at the same time.

19

What is recycling?

Many things we use can be made into new products when we are finished with them. The metal from old cars can be used to make new ones. This is called **recycling**.

Scrap metal from old cars can be melted down and used again.

What can we recycle?

We can recycle paper, tin cans, glass, plastic, rags, wood, and electrical goods. Some recycled things can be sorted and put out with the trash. Others can be taken to recycling centers.

Garden recycling

If you have a garden you can recycle vegetable scraps into compost.

Compost is broken down vegetable matter. It puts the nutrients and richness back into the soil. You can turn fruit and vegetable peelings into compost.

Add compost to the soil when you plant things.

TalKing PoiNt

How do I know what I can recycle?

Many products are marked with a recycling symbol on them. This means they are made from materials that can be used again. It is important to recycle these things.

Can I recycle water?

Water can be recycled. You can use your bath water to water your plants. After a bath, let the water cool. Collect it in buckets to use on the plants. You can also save rainwater in large buckets. Make sure the buckets have lids so animals do not fall in.

Helping Earth

Did you know that saving energy and water where you live can help everyone on Earth? Everyone should try to save energy.

WORD WIZARD!
climate
Typical patterns of weather, recorded over a long period of time

What is global warming?

Fumes, or smoke, from vehicles, power stations, factories, and big farms pollute the air. These gases surround Earth. They raise the temperature and cause **global warming**.

dried up river bed

What is climate change?

Global warming is already changing Earth's climate. Soon some places will get stormier and wetter. Others will become drier and dustier, with little water.

Cleaning Earth

Some **organizations** work together to clean up Earth. Others help bring clean water to people. This woman is planting trees. Trees keep water in the soil. They help clean the air, too.

When you buy fruits and vegetables, look on the labels to see where they were grown.

Why should we eat food grown locally?

Supermarkets sell food grown in many different parts of the world. This food has to be moved from one place to another by trucks, ships, or planes. These use a lot of fuel. By eating food that is grown close by, less fuel is needed. If we use less fuel and power Earth will be a cleaner place.

What can I do to help the environment?

If you follow the tips in this book you will help the **environment**. Watch when you use electricity or other fuels. Try to think of ways you can use less. Recycle as many things as you can.

23

Glossary

appliances Small machines that do work in the house

cell A small battery

destroy To ruin completely

environment Earth around us, including the land, sea, air, and living things

filtered A liquid, such as water, which has been strained to remove harmful things in it

geothermal The heat from inside Earth

global warming A rise in the temperature of our planet

hydroelectric Making power from moving water

organization A group of people who believe in the same thing and work together to help support their belief

pollute To poison land, sea, or air with waste or chemicals

power station A big factory where electricity is made

radiation The giving out of rays, such as light or heat. Some of the rays given out by the materials used in nuclear reactions may be dangerous

recycling Processing worn out or discarded materials, so they can be used again

renewable Something that can be replaced or never run out

reservoir A large lake or tank used for storing liquids such as water

resource Something that helps. Natural resources are materials that come from Earth such as water and fuels

turbine A spinning motor that is used to generate electricity

valuable Of great use or importance

ventilation Passing of air through an enclosed space, such as a house

Index